Angel Cloud Poetry III
The Jasmine of the Night

David P. Carlson

Order this book online at www.trafford.com
or email orders@trafford.com

Most Trafford titles are also available at major online book retailers.

Print information available on the last page.

ISBN: 978-1-4907-7454-1 (sc)
ISBN: 978-1-4907-7455-8 (hc)
ISBN: 978-1-4907-7453-4 (e)

Library of Congress Control Number: 2014917213

Trafford rev. 10/19/2018

 www.trafford.com
North America & international
toll-free: 1 888 232 4444 (USA & Canada)
fax: 812 355 4082

Contents

Acknowledgements

By David P. Carlson

Special thanks to Becky Campbell for her consistent support with her many talents that have made these poems artistically legible.

Also, of course, to my wife, Linda, many thanks for her patience and daily encouragements. Without her devotion, love, and faith the inspiration for each poem would have never been manifested on paper.

Finally without my salvation, (provided by the Ancient of Days, God the Father of all the ages, Creator of all that has ever existed) and without the ultimate sacrifice of His only begotten son, Jesus of Nazareth for the sins of all mankind all combined, His mercy, sacrifice and love (these His three essential elements) I would have no reason or compulsion to express any passion worth pursuing --- "all would be vanity".

Life Between the Lines
By David P. Carlson

Poetry, a series of written events all conspiring to force the reader to recall a multitude of people, places and things so remote (yet so greatly inhabited by the beauty of so many painful events) that they so unwillingly paint a portrait of themselves so vivid that reality yields to the divine awareness of a conscious serenity, so complex that all (so simply put) are sadly mundane; Unforeseen and suddenly this solitary life burst upon the scene, confronts the risings in his mind, then kneels to the descending light of time and grace, affirms the course, then steps across the line so quickly drawn; With a stuttering gasp and a choking hiss, he speaks the words, "Amen, so be it, so now it is." Now truth has been revived as it comes to light in one dark corner of his mind: there beneath the shadowed veil now reveals a man couched and pale, clad in a coat of mail; content to shun the light of the poet's pen. So now he stands, now to embrace the waiting hope for a life well spent, all within the realm of the poet's spin on a life within, never to be content to die again, all propelled by the tip of the poet's pen——
This book was written for one purpose and one purpose only, which is for you to view your life behind, yet through this thin veneer of words and phrases, stories and allegories, all created to blend from within (you the reader) personal considerations of specific recollections of times, (ill or well spent) – but now content to attempt to climb above your future's considerable mountains of compilations. These poems (as is life itself) without a purpose or a point are as trees without limbs or leaves, no trunk or bark, no roots or seeds to grow, could never become a shade for that next generation—please attempt to read, then bask in some related truth—Take a mental sabbatical and say, "That's what I'll do for the rest of my days"—and so is the fruit of enlightenment of so many trees of truth—all within your reach upon heaven's special ladders—each rung a book, each step a gate that swings forever wider, so as to view the world around and your place in life, three-score and six rungs higher.

The Miracle of Transformation

By David P. Carlson

In 1953 the Spirit of God drew me out of the pew and into the aisle and down to accept my Lord's salvation. I don't remember what Brother (Rev. Lunsford) said, but I'll never forget the joy of that nine year old boy.

---Nineteen years later---

I often wonder what Brother (Rev. C.C. Hurst) thought that night when the doorbell rang---probably, "Who can that be at this time of night," or "what major problem am I about to face this time?" Hesitantly he opened the door and I heard him say, "Can I help you?" and then, "Oh, David, what's the problem?" I had been at his church before (he immediately recognized sister Bozman's granddaughter's bar-room boyfriend---ME!!) Well, there we were; myself, my girlfriend, and my best friend, J.B White, standing there on the porch. We had been arguing about if God was real over a couple of six-packs (or more maybe). I'm sure he could smell the beer on my breath, but believe it or not, he said, "Let's go over to the church and talk this over. It wasn't long that he cut to the chase and said, "David, do you want ot give your life back to the Lord tonight and receive him as Lord and Savior?" I said, "Yes, Pastor Hurst, I do." I was immediately completely sober. He then led me in the sinner's prayer and that was that. My friend J.B. was stunned, to say the least, and, no doubt, highly disappointed in me. Brother Hurst asked J.B., "How about you son?" J. B. stormed out with an unlit cigarette dangling from his mouth; I think I even heard him curse a little. We had been friends for at least ten years, but everything changed that night. We never really ever spoke again to each other up to the time he died about 15 years later.

Well, I began to display, at that point, a major change. Church was my life and God began to mold me into a new man. I married my girlfriend, (sister Bozman's granddaughter) who had 3 children from former marriages already. Before we married in God's presence, one night he spoke to me to the effect, "I've given you a new life, now will you have a problem with raising these 3 children as your own?" I said, "Yes, Lord, I will do it."

Well, things got better and better. We bought a small trailer (my parents were a bit skeptical about me taking on such a responsibility). But finally they came around and supported my decision since they were so thrilled that I had changed from a bar-room brawler to a Bible-toting Christian. They were totally convinced something wonderful had happened and said "Amen!"

-----But the best was yet to come!!!-----

One night I took JoAnn and Mary (ages 3 and 6) to a church revival. That night I told Brother Hurst, "I know I'm saved and things are going great, but something is missing. He prayed for me. After the service we headed home. On the way, it seemed the Lord brought to my remembrance an incident that had happened years before my God-drawn conversion. We had been partying, drinking, drugging, etc, on a little beach in Bayside, TX. I had a little boat that me and J.B. had built (a red, all wood, flat-bottom boat). It wasn't real big but it was heavy. At one point I ended up on that boat by myself. Everybody else was up on the shore. I kind of panicked when I realized it was almost dark and I was pretty high and I was drifting out into the bay. Everybody thought that was pretty funny, but it wasn't. I could have ended up all night drifting to who knows where. When that dawned on me, I grabbed the anchor and threw it in—guess what? It wasn't tied on to the boat's rope!! I only had one option—I grabbed the rope and jumped in the water that came just below my chest. I began the long, arduous task of pulling that boat back to the shore which took about what seemed hours. But finally I made it to the shore. Everybody got a big laugh out of that. As I was thinking about that experience going up on the 13th block of N. Ave. D that night, it was like God said, "that boat was all those sins I have forgiven you for" —then I saw God cut the rope!! I was free from that great enormous weight, and friend, I went nuts!!! It was a rush I had never experienced!! I took the girls home and told my wife what had happened and that I had to find brother Hurst and let him know too. I went by my parent's house and literally burst in and told them that something wonderful had happened!! I think they thought I was on drugs, drunk or just gone crazy again. Next morning I was still filled with that wonderful anointing that has never, to this day, subsided.

Well, forty-two years have come and gone and I've been blessed with 3 children of my own. I've been through many trials including my wife's death in 1996 of leukemia.

Then in 1998 God blessed me with Linda, and life has never been better!! Old things passed away forty-two years ago, and all things just keep getting newer!!!

Winter's Hand

I stand in winter's robe, clutching warmth where I can.
I reach to feel the cold night wind
Tears on winters face I touch
Her sadness holds me, clutching warmth where she can.
I take her hand, I understand
Her tears splash, then turn to ice
A winters night has found a friend.

--David Paul Carlson

As Published by
The National Library of Poetry

Abigail-a Source of Joy
Angel

By David P. Carlson

Abigail-a Source of Joy
Angel

By David P. Carlson

Sweetly silent this tender life has slipped away,
passing peacefully along her days as a springtime
song of praise to the Lord of the great beyond.
This soul-full child, a melody as pure as a gentle
wind upon this place of her eternal rest, now left
to sway upon countless waves of heaven's
symphonic melodies, her spirit strolls through care-
free days with her friends, the angels, there to
guide her on all her ways. As this resplendent
angelic child resides there within her songs she
hums a pleasant tune for Mom and Dad to hear
there within their dreams.
With a perfect pirouette she spins, then turns
again to skip along to find a place to count the
days when her life will once again meet those
cherished ones, her family and those future friends
on that bright and sun-bathed day, where they all
together can sing as one in perfect harmony the
song of the redeemed.

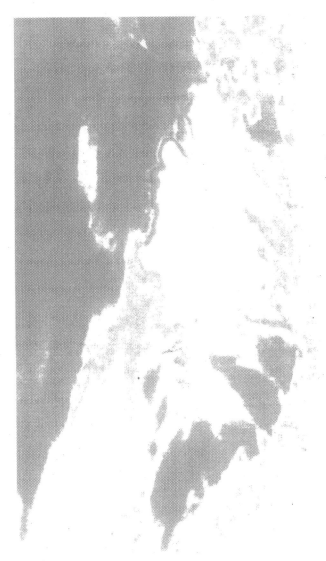

Angel Cloud

By David P. Carlson

Angel Cloud

By David P. Carlson

*Misty vapors merge, then mingle as a trailing wisp from her
rainbow-laced wedding gown; angel cloud then serenely
drifts across in stark contrast to the blues and greens and
garnished golds of the sunlit knolls of yesterday, today and
forever.*

*Her presence tolls, enunciating a place in the time where
poetic lines will be inscribed upon a mind to reflect the
vision there for countless souls, there to be enthralled at the
sight of this heavenly radiance of her multi-colored glow; a
divine reflection from the promised one who set the bow
there in creation's days of old, who proclaimed the hopes and
dreams of yesterday, today and forever. As he swirled the
clouds, he donned his hand with a satin brush to slash the
sky with a grand array of illuminated prism shades galore,
to forge the supreme depiction of the angle cloud in all her
splendid glory. Now I say, "she was a sight to behold in her
classic, wind-drawn surrey."*

Angel in the Cloud—to God Be the Glory

Is She Relevant?

By David P. Carlson

She is relevant because each poem mirrors society, from coal miners to the Boston bombing, from wars abroad to your battles deep within, from the finger of God to the pointed sword at the devil's head. With all that this book is, it screams "It's not in theory, it's all relevant!!"

Many books, in some ways, mimic others. This book, when it was finished (even though I wrote it), made me wonder from whom it was I stole it. But then I recognized the true Author is truly like no other—the Holy Spirit, rightly noted, penned each word because to God I give the glory, and God has deemed that relevant to the angel in the cloud for me to meet the angels of Revelation.

A Penthouse View of the Last Days

By David P. Carlson

Since all the encroachments of escalating darkness throughout all the descending centuries since time began, these Last Days still contain, though diminished, a strain of hope I call the isthmus lane which runs between Veracity's efficiency apartments and the perfidy acute-occult townhouse dwellings along the esplanade of Satanic Avenue and Demonic Drive; this scenic route along the shore is better known to those that dwell therein as the only way to drive through the storms of Christendom to avoid the chance that they might join. Now the byways have been paved by the terroristic tar of barbarism, trafficking winds around the curbs and lines of the interstate of human souls. All life has been exploited—biblical principles—prophecies and all those holy covenants are the only lanes still left to connect this Christian isthmus to the stars—our home and God alone.

This final esplanade along the shore of eternity has turned out to be nothing more than the earth's back door, an anathema where fools may dwell, void of wit or cleverness. So here, there within their final domain these nimble-fingered identity thieves jeer, then flaunt their ill-gotten gains, having done all they can to authenticate their claim to fame as their name proclaimers, "The defiant ones". So now, as their days wind up and down they slow their pace, and as time expires they settle down in their pre-assigned resting place, there to hang their hats at the tavern's inn, better known in this world below as the leper's den, --a cozy little colony growing up in leaps and bounds with an equally nauseating chorus of groans and frantic sounds.

(over)

Limp and twisted so describes their minds, bent so as to embrace the philosophy of Epicurus who believed that pleasure is the chief and utmost aim in life to gain, but unbeknownst to him another wise man said, "put a knife to the throat if a man be given to appetite," which reminds me of another tasteless and hopefully the last production of gloom and doom, a box-office hit and its final run at a world premiere.

So—here to proudly introduce this classic play, "The Old Grim Reaper", to describe every scene of a total eclipse of eternal life, day by day. "I, the Grim Reaper say, yes, I will, and how glad I am to introduce this darling cast, all draped in various forms of mass destruction; now how about a hand for the devil's crowd and their daunting last brigade." What a spectacular and memorable, but sad conclusion of a world whose hopes and dreams all hinge, and ultimately depend on Medicaid and Dairy Queen.

Now as the world returns as it was before the shout, "Let there be light!" you hear the cry of the multitudes all slated to return again to the dark corners of the universe. Total extermination, total evacuation from this blackened crust we call our molten earth, that's all that's left to entertain the world's profane, insane, inane, those bound in chains, all huddled in this bloody field of carnage where hopes and dreams have been reduced to ash and white-hot dust, (a final epigram without the wit), there to ponder in the soot and sludge of the bottomless pit—this finial esplanade you can avoid by a simple choice—so stay at home and serve the Lord—enjoy your view from your penthouse suite atop a higher calling.

A Temple's Steeple—Just a Point In View
By David P. Carlson

Temple's steeples spike the sky from coast to coast extending high above, through those glowing redwood cinders, dancing upward from those Sequoia martyrs, back wood mesquite, men of morals, joining in are those piney woods of contemporary forests, steeped in Christendom's Ridge, but commentaried versions of Christian universities, all ascending from the land below, all set ablaze by a volcano of civilian's civil and mental anthropoidic unrest and resentfulness, to then again be conjured up at a later date in some backstreet amphitheater to crank and bend those steeples down, to slash and chop those postulate points that permeate, then penetrate their scale-like skin: now resistance to them has always been excelled by Godly men with didactic tack, with such a verbal thrust it unlooses the fetters from the hearts of men and women, boys and girls who claim "in God they trust".

The enemy's ultimate task is this, to amend those truths within those sermonettes of so-called exhortations by men on high (those gray-bearded ones, schooled by celebrities and their countless groupie friends of anthropology) that probe their lies into the heavens with another set of pernicious temple's steeples of pines and needles.

Now the gist of all of this needs not to be revised, transposed, contrived or compromised, so then be deemed a perverted form of veracity (herecisty! so charged in some religious forums of duplicity), but truly this well-documented dominant creed does demand the cross on top should be displayed and plainly seen as an eternal and God-penned theme, for without the cross there would be no point to guide the way, nor challenge for us to tread across that swirling and swollen Jordan River of pride to the banks of Eternal Love, there atop those steeple's peaks there upon the other side, a point well taken to the Cross where there the tip was stained in red by the blood He shed to emphasize our so-called common and mundane steeples pointing to the skies.

Beyond the Generational Gap

By David P. Carlson

This generation chants peace on earth with paradigmal
slants, leaning on with each inflection toward the garbed cry
of suicidal insurrection—although vague, more or less, still
they well describe what they strive to represent as the path to
attain the plan for legal social status. Political winds unfurl
their flags to the dismay of many bewildered citizens. What
is this flag they dare to fly above this nation's hallowed
ground—nothing more than a counterfeit of what was once
held dear—how paradigmatic, totally driven by another
culture's instincts to be furiously ambiguous, yet they still
retain the name "a paradigm of shame or blame" however
your inflections are applied,—a literary algorithm sifting
through this plethora of symbolic words to describe their
despicable acts,to enhance a so-called paragon of the piano-
man brought to the highest strato-sphereal plain—there to
grapple for all to see the lowest of all degrees, the mesopause,
ninety kilometers above the mesosphere, any more would
exceed the boundaries of endless peace in those outer limits of
supersonic fears.

Those past generations that once chanted for affinity with
God, now seem faded under continuous conjecture of liberal
confederates, but alas, the trumpet sounds, fading faith
rebounds to disgorge the prose, to retain the rhyme of poetic
chimes as the congregation of the resplendent redeemed rise
beyond the boundaries of the mesopausic ridge, to escape the
chants of dying men, driven by the paradigm of their own
dissentions from grace and glory, all conjoined with no
further purpose than to receive for lack of compassion—
thirty-nine lashes on a continual daily basis.

Biblical Poetry (Glory)

Arranged by David P. Carlson (King James Version)

Lev. 9:6, 11, 23, 24

V6 And Moses said, This is the thing which the LORD commanded that ye should do: and the glory of the LORD shall appear unto you. V11 And the flesh and the hide he burnt with fire without the camp. V23 And Moses and Aaron went into the tabernacle of the congregation, and came out, and blessed the people: and the glory of the LORD appeared unto all the people. V24 And there came a fire out from before the LORD, and consumed upon the altar the burnt offering and the fat: which when all the people saw, they shouted, and fell on their faces.

I Kings 9:8-9

And at this house, which is high, every one that passeth by it shall be astonished, and shall hiss; and they shall say, Why hath the LORD done thus unto this land, and to this house? V9 And they shall answer, Because they forsook the LORD their God, who brought forth their fathers out of the land of Egypt, and have taken hold upon other gods, and have worshipped them, and served them: therefore hath the LORD brought upon them all this evil.

John 12:46

I am come a light into the world, that whosoever believeth on me should not abide in darkness

Branches

By David P. Carlson

Green and thin now equates to trembling lusts of chlorophylling
gel within the veins of leaves from their long extended stems and
branches. The relentless gusts of winter's breath bends then twists
till all seems lost, all is tossed from side to side till the wind
collides, buckles and then subsides again. Motionless, the limbs
silently weep and groan, as the tear-like sap flows from those
countless leaves and splintered twigs they once caressed (but now
sadly are bereaved) as their seed-rich stems, all now strewn
by God, there to be whisked away by another late December
breeze.

Brine Foam Upon the Shore

By David P. Carlson

Through oceans of time and space it seems I catch a glimpse of
your worried face peering out from behind your chin on knees
across the waves of a rising tide to the distant shores of yesterday;
As a salty gust of wind and mist shower you with (as you might
pessimistically describe) minute rocks called sand, I see you
hesitate, then step into the waves. Cold is the foaming brine—
some would count each wave as years, some would say they depict
your fallen tears, but I will say,
"Lift up your eyes a little higher to view the source of waves and
that ocean of your endless unborn days."

My prayer for you, my dear, is that you will return back to the
shore and once again confess him as your Lord of Lords, and in
that moment you'll see he'll come and leave his love and peace like
brine foam upon your youthful shore for you and yours; never to
receed, always present as the vast and endless sea of eternity.

Divine Design

By David P. Carlson

Though thoughts compressed in riddles, then guided
through a maze of endless walls of literary vines and
flowers, all draped in the premise that all men search
for their own divine design: who you are is summarized
by what you find concealed between the lines of life's
poetic rhyme that connects directly with you alone. As
positive depends upon the negative, so the mind and
soul finally find resolve to embrace the theme of a
continual falling, then rising and overcoming of all of
life's onslaughts of disappointments by injecting God's
Word and promises into the wound until you see at last
the miracle of his divine design spread abroad through
you to future generations.

Dream Busters

By David P. Carlson

Like a blank piece of paper is this man and his mind, once filled with the hope he would eventually find that long sought treasure he buried so well and so deep in the sands of the past where the winds have since scattered all signs of the path he might have so carelessly left in the wake of his wrath. Now compelled by only his memories, he tells how he staked his claim in the dirt, he then so cunningly lined with his life's perfect work (so he affirms) so worthily priceless he vigorously boasts is the ultimate cost of all his so well-deserved trophies, accomplished honors and goals: his claim was his fame you can instantly tell by his half-hearted smirk he thought he had hidden so well: surprisingly to me, there in the trash, he furiously retrieved that old crumpled up map of his long lost mine to again be revived by the sight of that mountain he would again be tempted to climb: now there in the mine with his arms and hands set in an akimbo-type of recline (his symbol of pride) he gathers his gold and jewels untold to be groomed as the grandest prize of all times for all to behold; his sparkling diamonds all priced at great worth of which, soon he thinks, all will be viewed by the great men of this earth! But sorely and painfully obvious were those stones set in rows, elegantly laid in perfect array, so starkly unnatural the question from within them begins to unfold—could this be that blank piece of paper, this shell of a man to be lead so astray that a handful of rocks could be the worth of the lot of his deed that he has so unfortunately already paid?

(over)

Now all is not lost for our misguided friend, for the price of this lesson could be less than a yen.

Now with one slight adjustment (as a chiropractor may say) let's dull the peak of his grief by applying my suggested suggestion with a new set of treasures to seek.

Let go of your map, give up your gold, turn to the source of all treasures untold—

Return to the Lord—through those tunnels you'll find ; deep within those recesses of forgiveness where therein lies that rich sense of peace where there he'll fulfill all your needs plus his blessings caressing all your life's most cherished collections of life-giving seeds. All that is required is then to simply say, "Lord, I believe, show me the way."

Elliptic Rose

By David P. Carlson

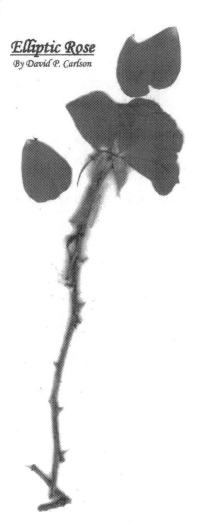

Elliptic Rose

By David P. Carlson

Alone the rose sways and bobs in perfect time with her friend the
sympathetic wind, there to be enjoined with their affirimities; he's
there to help caress her sadness she must feel to be the elliptic rose,
alone and tethered to her leafless stem high above the ground
without her leaf embroidered shroud; she knows the wind would
help her if he could, but without her leaves she has no beauty to
behold: now a rose by any other name is still not as sweet as the
leaves that hold her natural lusters bound, that come alive to entice
the petals, to join together, then blossom forth to release the scent
that defines her special fragrance, an essence to be enjoyed there far
above the leaves and far-reaching, bending stems.

Snip, snap, the enemy of her soul separates, eclipsing her leaves of
youthfulness, the memories of the days when she was just a bud
upon the stem of so many yesterdays! Elliptic rose sheared and
pruned of all her dignity, placed within an artificial vase, all set in
lines and rows. In her natural state, her insectic world denies her of
her leaves of green, now bronzed, now brown and speckled on the
ground——these leaves have eyes for there to gaze up tragically to
behold those wilted petals fluttering to the land below. But yet in
truth her true bud has yet to bloom, in death the elliptic rose with
one last breath has strength to gasp, then with one raspy whisper
say, "This, of all my days and now to this one I do succumb, I do
concede my life to cease, in all of this, I still do truly miss all my
cherished leaves."

Evil Paladin "The Grand Scammer"
By David P. Carlson

His duplicity emerges from a quiet and meek slightly humble and apparently
compliant frame of a man to arise abruptly as a cumulonimbus cancerous mass in the
northern skies, darkened by a charging hoard of swirling emotions just beyond the
curvature of his own horizons. This master obtuse deceiver consoles the trodden-
down only to tangle up their moments of despair and desperation with perilously,
profane verbal connotation of all their hopes and anxious expectations.
Their spirits were captivated by his grand disguise of perfidiousness and contorted
versions of perverseness, slightly bent and sculptured by his holy, pious arrogance,
perceived to be the enigma prince of tall, dark, and mysterious, master romancer of
the "holly in the woods" lying, dying novel steeped in science-fiction data, marinated
in a poetic soup of ludus love, with his own sadistic connotations.
From his chair, their director beacons them to review the script, dress the part, then
sip from the golden cup. His deadly dredge, so to become the ones, the enigma man's
queens of solitude in the infamous darked back stage forest of that immortal world,
all draped in the endless pain of death and sorrow.
Their parts in this Romeo, Jonah, and Juliet tragedy they so desperately desired to
play now welcomes them to their rewards at center-stage, to then to their surprise-
just one solitary line to say "I relent to not one prayer to pray". (Scratch romances) –
the part demands a sacrifice of only common sense- when only now when the play
concludes can they comprehend the enigma man's final and remarkably simple scam,
even a child can understand his demand to purge the words of truth and love through
a maze of mirrored glass to then appear absurd to those desperate hoards of rare but
faithful congregated protagonistic wanna-be's, there to emerge atop life's horizons,
there to confront the chair where the director of this disaster sits to welcome home his
begotten cast for one last curtain-call before the next final and far less alacritous
eternal intermission---
Now forgive me for this tragic end---so let me recommend salvation's alternative, a
well-plotted plan where Jesus Christ will preside as your new director and CEO,
where all your future hopes and dreams may flow, to stroll across that emberal stage
to receive your golden crown, where never ever is that curtain allowed to come
crashing down, or to be drawn to mute that wild applause of countless fulgent
throngs of welcoming apologistic angels around the sides of God's golden throne, all
there for your eternal and forever certain curtain-call from God, "Hey, come on in,
make yourself at home!"

Final Destination

By David P. Carlson

Destination, a box car noun, towed sinuously by two or three engine verbs up
Mt. Decision, there to abjectly and conjecturally steam up to the summit of a
place where dreams solidify, then settle down to suffer. Your destination
sometimes lags behind as your conscious mind winds around the endless tracks of
current events which lead in all directions. This noun called destination, though
not designated is oh so personality enunciated—as youth bends down to take
ahold those verbs emerge, then scamper through the forest, make fly the twigs
and leaves, the trees and shrubs have left behind—some destinations are but a
blur that one observes from afar or maybe from a car that plunges down, then
overturns through the curves and bends, through the guarding rails of twisted tin
to one more monumental crash before your face meets that wonderful safety
device called air in bags along with its shrapnel and splintered glass; you're
blown away into a comatose-like state, never again to recall the dates of births
of any of your closest kin—so is the end of so many unfortunate few that find
this scenario to be true and destined to be their final destination;
Life is so much better when your destination resonates precisely as a welcome
homing beacon, luming in the distant hills, pulsating with a resplendent glow,
always clear, never perfidious as the obscure, obtuse chorus of semantical riddles,
riddled with vain objectives that never truly lead to a fruitful God-honored
destination. A goal is more than civil rest or even more than just a test to pass.
The road to any worthy destination has at least a few complications wrapped in
butcher paper, no brilliant bow to be set aside, you only know that where your
name resides it will be written clear within your sight, there upon the map that
leads to that place you hope to soon arrive, there in God's New Creation on the
other side, there to settle in to enjoy the view of the past at last, from your newly
found, eternal, and final destination.

Flight Ninety-three

By David P. Carlson

Flight Ninety-three

By David P. Carlson

Her temples quiver, tremble, then sway from side to side like towering steeples in the wake of tornatic winds swirling in the black foreboding skies, all minimized by the stark approaching terror there visualized before her eyes of fleeting, evaporating memories of her closest kin and her own life so soon to end. Her contemplations rise, then fall, pierce through the morning rays to unveil a day of such voraciously correlated streams of repetitiveness, such a barrage of her reciprocating arteriolar aorta vibrations, so intense as to enhance the river of gushing emotions, all so furiously frightening it grips the heart to imagine the escalating horror that her reeling and bewildered mind and soul must have been forced to feel and see, trapped inside that fuselage of flight Ninety-three—all her plans of yesterday are now neatly stitched upon the fabric of those tear-laced cirrocumulus clouds outside her double-paned window sill, all embroidered by her tormented mind there within the shambles of her resonating family's memories, and as of yet, all forlorn, all too soon to be forgotten: -- then reaching in with heart in hand, she penned her heart-felt letter to those loved ones so soon to be left behind, all viewed and synchronized through her little window in the sky.

(over)

Some say, where was God on the tragic day? So let me attempt
to comfort your endless grief with one resplendent ray of hope—
God was there to calm her soul with a peaceful and loving hand
to hold on that day of sacrifice for God and country and this
nation's soul, all set and parenthesized by what that man said,
"Let's rock, let's roll"—a phrase so plain, but yet so bold.

Is this the end? I think not; for all those souls lost that day and
all those families' sadness, compounded by countless wrongs
untold, the bar was raised for this nation's goal to conceive a
plan to cleanse the land of marauding hordes of ruthless men like
Osama-bin-Laden. These senseless and brutal acts of war will
remind us all for evermore that no matter how high the steeples
tower to the sky, or how shrill the engines roar their terror
through our skies, none can ne'er compare the gratitude we feel
for those brave plenipotentiary souls that took that beleaguered
flight (Flight Ninety-three) down to the land below, to that
peaceful holy plot of ground of serenely rolling meadows there on
the Pennsylvania countryside, instead of downtown in our
nation's capitol to be laid to rest alongside our nation's pride
and our most-of-all most treasured phrase, "In God we trust".

Fool and the Storm
By David P. Carlson

Birds chatter in torrent weather?
What could it mean except fear or ignorance?
Does not the wind or driving rain or flashing lights or
bolts of thunder, curl their feathers, wrench their bodies
with thoughts of a violent end to their seemingly useless
lives?
Or is it merely a scene, seen through darting eyes,
watching closely and seeing nothing? So it is with some
men I know.

Free

By David P. Carlson

There is a man in prison in this world today—

There are no locks on the doors but in his mind he's still a slave. He may escape someday, he may even block the past.

He may walk in the sun and say at last I'm free.

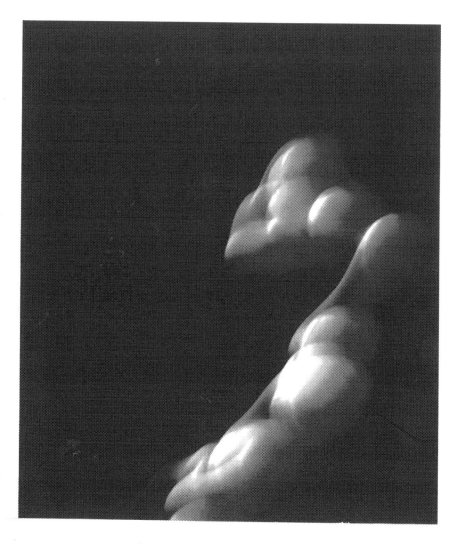

Galactic Time Blood Moon's Risings
By David P. Carlson

Galactic Time Blood Moon's Risings

By David P. Carlson

Rumbling thunder in the night, how courageous are those gathering clouds in early morning's light, there to cause a schism in the atmosphere; such is the swirling of God's celestial mass, so precise as if to point the way to that special day when light denied becomes the shroud across the blood moon's prophetic anno-domini face, there to be our constant meridian reminder of God's ephemeral moment there within translucent space when all of God's collected planets will align with their trailing stones of fire to be as stepping stones for God's elect to skip across as one to that blood moon's peneplain and there to see the Sea of Tranquility transformed from crimson red to virgin green, and then, there we be donned in robes of sky-like blues, bathed in that golden glow of interspace for God's royal introduction, to then behold the face of that ancient architect of all creation, his outer space of garden nebulas, clustered about as glowing clouds of dust and gases, all spread across that massive blue and black star-speckled canvas, so well foretold from fifteen-million light years away in that distant constellation.

Now as the story goes in that splendiferous southern pinwheel galaxy roams that old mythological three-headed serpent known as Hydra, huge, but lack of light, barely seen from afar, (understandably so, being armed with only seventeen less astronomical protagonistic soldier stars). So now in acronical manner, an acronically occurring event, transcending at the moment of life and death, from night to light, in panoramic retrospect looms Crux, also known as the Southern Cross, smaller but among the brightest in the southern hemisphere, only four stars strong! Also there, nestled snuggly beneath the Coal Sack Nebula is that brilliant jewel-box cluster; herein lies God's celestial message, sealed within the heavens, that dominant southern crux of that resplendent cosmic cross now lies embedded as a Biblical heel upon the head of Hydra, herein for all to see that two thousand years ago that star struck three-headed snake, of all astronomical treacheries has received his final blow to reduce his reign as prince of the air to nothing more than another super nova remnant of yesterday, now held in God's utmost distain. Such a grand array of distant stars within the cosmic dust, then displayed just for us there on high to warn the world of an impending end of galactic time. Now another end-time sign a little closer home, so now look up and watch the sky and know "your redemption draweth nigh", signified by another blood moon rising.

God's Way

By David P. Carlson

Well, now it's God's Way that we know that what we understand to be our Holy Bible, that's of spirit, not of man; Lord and it's God's Way that we be taught, the power of his word, and it's God's Way that we live every day what we've learned. Lord, and it's God's Way that we be spread like the flowers in the field on the green grass of Jesus beneath the blue skies of God's will. Lord, then it's God's Way that we grow up like the redwoods in the land, there by the brook of Jesus to stand all acts of man. Lord, and it's God's Way that our branches reach out for human souls and gather for the Master a bouquet of red, blue and gold—golden souls. Lord, and it's God's Way that we come through Jesus to the throne and praise God for God's Way, 'cause.....God's Way is the way home.

You know sometimes it's God's Way that we feel all alone, but you know that's just God's Way of craving faith, in our sometimes' hearts of stone. And you know, sometimes it's God's Way that fear is something we really feel, but you know, that's just God's Way of tempering strength into our faith and then through us, God can heal. Just remember back through God's Way and that step you just couldn't take alone, and remember it was God's Way that gave you that faith and the strength and courage to go on. Oh, if we could just live everyday God's Way, everyday would be a stepping stone, and everyday we'd be a little stronger, and everyday we'd be just a little closer home.

Gone in Time
By David P. Carlson

There I saw a painted sky—two lives stayed to see it.
The lights we saw were gone in time, but to us we had
their image.
We touched and weaved the meaning, then saw and
felt their leaving,
I tried to stop, hold back the times, but forever time
was gone, even before the ending.

Guy Fawke's Protégé
The Diatribe Rapscallion Lion (the Anti-Christ)
By David P. Carlson

(guy n 1: MAN 1a: FELLOW 2: PERSON. Word history—Nov. 5 is a holiday in England, and people celebrate it by setting off fireworks and lighting bonfires. Human likenesses made of tattered clothes stuffed with hay or rags are burned on the bonfires. The holiday is called Guy Fawkes Day for a 17th century man who played a leading role in a plot to blow up the British Parliament buildings. Fawkes managed to hide 20 barrels of gunpowder in the cellars of the buildings. However, the plot was discovered before Fawkes could carry out his plans. He was seized and later put to death. The human likenesses burned to celebrate the failure of Guy Fawkes' plot came to be called guys. The use of the word was extended to similar figures and then to a person of strange appearance or dress. In the U.S. the word came to mean simply "man" or "fellow" and in time came to be used for a person of either sex [named for Guy Fawkes 1570-1606 English criminal].
(From Webster's Intermediate Dictionary © 1986 by Merriam Webster, Inc.)

As a lion's roar perks up the vigilant shepherd's ears, the
sheep are scattered, sent scampering through the fields of dark
intimidating hills and shadows. Diatribe well describes this
lion's constant arising pernicious tone in every sentence
(derived, then contrived by this bureaucratic rapscallion type
of Guy, a Guy Fawkes plotting wanna-be) for maximum
collateral damage to the common man and to all that hear his
rambling, beaconing and hecklings, all coinciding with his vile
display of mesmerizing the local yokels at their annual
Christmas plays and parties: well, it seems this is the key to
all human conversations since time arrived in the back lands
of those long-forgotten blacked holes of endless space where
there still is stored galaxies of abundant grace for times as
these, end of time, end of days.
His strategy is that victory goes to the most vociferous orator,
thus unlocks the door (as we all know, only one may enter in),
but then, when to his chagrin he miserably fails to achieve his
goal to trample the source of such lethal confrontations, he
slithers back into his hole to plan another bold and sinister
plot to overthrow those innocent lambs, so lost and so cold;

(over)

so now with many final exacting demands this kingly schlemiel swells with pride to think his foe would shrink and fold, then cower down to listen with bated breath his diatribe-able exhortations, so soon he thinks to be recorded by this next generation with admiring poetic flair, garnished with a rare but colorful facsimile of the words he's spoken there: so beneficial they say, so stimulating it extracts the senses so that when confronted by so many confirming attacking facts his eidetic memory decides to forget what he's talking about. Between his lips and brain lie a vast expanse so designed for calculating his next response to the world around (draped in chaos and devastation) to spew out mostly useless information for his robot congregation with their cannibalistic tendencies and unprecedented lack of patience and consistencies. Obviously his diatribe-able personal resemblance of communication has broken off the key within the lock to dash the hopes of men that dare to span the gap, and once again communicate man to man, but this man has defiled himself by his futile attempt to confront the Shepherd of the flock with nothing more than his verbal, inimical arrogance along with his diabolical machination that in turn his beloved dubious gains gain only an angry stare of intense despite from the one and only God of this his cosmic plane and universe.

Now with one stroke of divine rebuke he's stricken mute, left with only one sense to hear the words spoken from before the throne, "You have been judged and found wanting!", the last salutation from the master of the one-sided conversation.

King Gull

By David P. Carlson

Two circles, islands unmanned, with his feathers picked and cleaned, his
glassy black eyes then dart with instinct's protecting culture...or maybe
with emotions, or is it devotion——maybe human feelings flow and fly
with King Gull. Who knows, not I?

King Gull searches among his subjects——reflect his obligations and
dominates his objectives——King Gull has earned his position and his
subjects obey his decisions——with chest bared, feathers back, he struts
among the citizens——KING GULL UNDISPUTED!!

The sea, the blue-white sky, the breeze that ruffles feather, ALL KING
GULL SENSES. With his kingdom unmolested, he must feel rewarded,
his duties stand fulfilled. Serenity's peace brings thought of his lofty
world, gliding with nature, his natural gift, lands below his resting place,
the sky above his frolicking playground.

HIS KINGDOM STANDS UNMOLESTED

A humming omen, a far-off fear no human yet foreseen——distance has no
meaning, the speed of sound is but a reeling him King Gull knows as
fear——then the distant fear coils out, strikes King Gull's ears —
unknowing he faces a bird gigantic, a crisis he never knew sweeps into
King Gull's vision. Then silent is his kingdom and defenseless is his
fear——He sees the faces of fear upon his subjects.

He knows his actions are within the eyes of every member. With silent
courage he reflects his kingly state, then collects his instinct's gifts and
call's his leaders forth——He speaks, "Take all and hide beneath the brush,
home is in the path of death. Here we stay, I will tell you when to go".
(Three days pass and King Gull waits). From within the brush, he fears
the sky as death——His subjects wait his decisions (to the mass he speaks).
In our worlds of air you've seen an awesome creature——across the bay our
duties lay unattended—— Our fear must be forsaken for across the bay is
our home, our beginning, our end, and if our end must come while trying,
then our homes must be worth the dying.

Life and Inspiration

By David P. Carlson

Inspiration is something that comes without an official announcement. Catapulted by either a personal or world event the subject unfolds in flight, then sails furiously to the ground. The trick is in the landing— the landing is the inspiration that God has charted – a safe and prosperous adventure from the take-off to the hangar.

Life Held Golden
By David P. Carlson

Look, a child held still in a golden frame—
he seems so blue, so true—maybe innocence covers
his face.

His stare calls us to remember when he had no sin.

In time he sees; his dark eyes flash with life. His
body moves, his soul stands never changing.

His portrait tells his story. His parents tell of his
life—his pain lies within him. His childish face
leaves no trace—leaves no hint of why he changed
in time.

Lofty
By David P. Carlson

Upon my cloud in the sky of life my tempered taste
seems satisfied by a candle's light in which my eyes
have fixed a path. But the storms of life and their
seasons grow forever tense, forever longer through the
surging rage of time; passing years breed collected duties
till the sky is filled with lighted kites which all string
neatly back to me.
So the task of life must have such burdens, but the
burdens of life cannot be my only task;
For the light I seek has a candle's glow; and its
stringless tie to my searching mind, is its salvation.

Looking Down into the Pit I Stumbled Into Fifty Years Ago

By David P. Carlson

Ca-choo—my lasting breath—all in one—my life stands still, my eyes lay open
and still. Pray, call out? Throw my life's despair on stronger limbs?
Be merciful in my deliverance, cast down my robe of death, be merciful in my
sight. Oh, how long have I to wait?—how long does mercy last before I die? I
plead one lasting gift, just one. Break down the walls of mercy and deliver me
once more another world to wring my face and shed one lasting tear.
All hail those who stand before me, for they speak truths venom's blood.
BEGINNING THE AWAKING FROM THE DREAM.
How meekly I slur my words, how sweetly I whine. Is not this true in this
world we live? Sainted cares live only in our own bewildered minds. What are
cares which have only one beginning, one end? Spare me such a tattered role in
such a dismal play, leave me to grant my wish— Oh, thine is so unworthy—a
care, a feeling a part of one's own soul, are they not worthy thoughts? In hell
they leave me not even an ash, not even one speck of light, they go not there.
So why can't I be in heaven where one knows such worth. Why? Because I am
here, we are here, we are in hell. Our lives are myths, a fool's bewildered mind.
There are those who remember, but not in a memory's way. Could it be I say?
Have I found a curse I dare not know? God help me if I have. Is this one step
down? Or two, or three? Where are we in time, have we lived and died, lived
and died, given another chance in lines, in rows, down, down, down till we
moan in gutters, gasp for breath, hold our sides and scream. All hail thee
something—Squeeze me one last time, for in the next life I will be born in hell
itself. HALF REALITY TRANSCENDS THE NIGHT.
THE FIRST NIGHT IN JAIL I feel the sweat, I feel the cell, I cast my head
down in the night and realize I've been here an eternity engulfing three hours.
It's night, my first night, my only night in jail since I was conceived. Then I
remember—there was a year, a whole year, that no one can tell me about, say
about, nothing about that year. Maybe this is not my first, my real mother,
(whoever you are, were maybe now), I don't know,--maybe she was in jail
while I lay asleep within her. Could it be? Imagine a whole year passing from

Dearborn, Michigan, to San Antonio, Texas, (where I was adopted)and not a
hint of how or why. The thought has always left me unknowing, wondering
and making excuses for those who cast me out. The wondering comforts me at
last, for only such a thought could now when my adopted mother sleeps
peacefully at home, not aware her son's soul leans slowly toward times
guillotine death. The tortures I bring march to her closer and closer with every
second, and with the morning, the day looks cheerful to her. Now down to her
daily tasks, and still the marching comes closer. The tromping, (she surely heard
in the distance of her dreams) thundered on. The hum grows to a devastating
peak, then the bugle sounds and the blade lays bloody, cursed and abandoned. I
FEEL HER MOAN, I FEEL IT ALL, I CRY AND GASP A BREATH.
That morning, that slashing morning I knew my mother was dead. I
WHIMPER HUMBLY, I WANT TO RISE AND GO CRY OUT AT HER
GRAVE, BEG A PRAYER TO HER, FOR HER,--but I cannot, I am in jail.
I cannot go, I must sit and think. Where is glory at the moment you destroy all
possibility of a normal life? There hidden I suppose, also hidden in the rubble
is the definition of glory, all wrapped up in each of us. So the morning came,
the blade fell and the cries brought a stable mood and the mood in time was
bearable as is with repetition, repetition of the same thoughts over and over
until all thoughts are thought, all lives are hit and we all attempt to stagger to
reality and resume our former forms.
RECALLING THE MORNING I THOUGHT WAS A BAD DREAM,
THEN REALIZING IT'S REALITY. The door opens,(breakfast in hell). In
lines we wait, we eat, for we must live even though we live for nothing (just to
live for the sake of living must hunt men's souls). Silently we trudge forward
and then we sit, we feast, we whimper, we gag on our descendants gaze. Here
we are, grounded as a family of thieves, drunkards, smugglers, and all of us
slaves of our neglect, all neglected, all purified by distant thoughts of a peaceful
time. Such an hour in such a crowded mist and in it all time stands blurred, not
awake, but partly, then more, then more. Ah, yes, I remember now, - O, God, I
thought it was just a bad dream I'd waken from and say, man that sure was a
bad scene, but the dream has just begun and you know it after about the third

gulp of greasy coffee, (thrown in as a luxury, but really as an awake call to the hell we live). The mumbling of savage men (like bombs you hear far away) reassure my awaking. Too soon your ears, your eyes and all sensations quiver with life and all defense mechanisms lay slain by reality.

Morning Jail

The morning sun rises slowly with essence as its name. Like Satan himself, he bears down, rays drooping in like benefits from hell, (cordial openings for boiling water). I soak in heated swirls only the devil could have stirred so swiftly. Sweat pours from every pore and every breath proceeds thoughts wound in gloom, physical and mental yokes all harnessed in the seclusion of this cage I live. I think maybe sleep will rescue me from this day but such a trip would take too long and on what mobile thought, from what source of power could propel with enough thrust to drive me to oblivion from reality's stinging heat from body and soul? No chance of a Buddhist's trance or a switch to be turned off when thoughts rage out of control,- so the battle of sane and sanity pants on. So I keep thinking and now I realize,- go ahead and think, you can't win- and the moment I stop fighting I realize, I snap, I think I must do anything of the smallest torture. Let's see——REMEMBERING THE ARREST IN LAREDO last night we were so screwed, so fiendishly clever to hide those four bulging sacks in the innocent looking wheel with the devil-may-care stamped clearly on each lug nut. I realize now how obvious it was that all of the other wheels were innocently dirty except the one left front tire, and that's what the man said, "just take off the left front tire and bust it down Mack," – and there it was. That guy at the service station didn't care. He was just making fifty cents to take the tire off. If he only knew what he was doing.

So there I stood partially in shock, partially mindfully sane.

WHAT DID I DO? WHO? WHAT? I'VE EATERN WHILE ASLEEP BUT WHAT HAVE I EATEN? I'VE EATEN WHAT THEY GAVE ME, THEY GAVE ME NOURISHMENT, BUT WHY SHOULD THEY CARE.

Then it begins, I remember everything, not quite everything, but enough. All these men, they are all Mexicans——I don't care, but who will I explain to, who

will understand, who will care? In it all I'd forgotten my friends where here too. I look in and out, over and around till, Hah! There they are—
In one breath I let out a sick sort of laugh gush out as I see JB sitting there like Humpty Dumpty slaughtering a big old sweet roll. I wonder about that. How could he be so hungry, like he didn't even notice he was in jail. I seem to be expecting at any moment for him to finish his rolls and reach for his coffee, sipping it slowly as his eyes fall on his surroundings. Then he slowly lowers his cup, sets it softly on the metal table and turns slowly looking at the horrible sight—then jumps to his feet, holds his head and yells, "Hey, Man, What in the Hell?", but none of this, he seems at home here-- Oh, well, with a few more quick glances I spot Terry sitting there like in a trance. He must be thinking about anything but food. Such guessing is agony. If I'm tempted to read minds, I have many other interesting, deep morals, code, answers and lies to probe into right here before me. At least forty men, all outcasts in their own ways, convicted by other laws more subtle than those that put them here. But so much for sidetrack now. A span of time must be paved by a laboring mind, (mine most assuredly) and I am ready. Bold statements make the humblest of men seek refuge.

Laredo Turmoil

THE DREAM FILLS MY CONSCIOUSNESS,-I snap, I crawl, I look up and study my surroundings-and then I a rise and wash my face. It was such a beautiful day too. I even felt good again after such a long, gasping, humble pleading, not pleading, but wondering, not wondering,--such an ordeal. I can't even seem to put my finger on the smallest muttering of my meager thoughts. Values seem trivial compared to my confusion. From the love of life to its trials, my paths have engaged in their own public stages. All who watch feel glorified by my witnessing. I have sinned before the eyes of man—now the shattering of lives and thoughts have subsided and sunk to the bottom—To them they feel rewarded and proud to sit in rose-tinted pulpits of purity for their pasts are far behind. REMEMBERING THE REALITY THAT BRINGS THIS STATE, THIS MIND relieved——Now I descend to and have descended from (what seems years ago, but really a month ago) that day not long ago in Laredo when the sacrifice to the guns of life (the sacred pigeons which fly above and protect our worldly goods but have not the wisdom to protect our trivial gloomy pleasures, thoughts, personalities and all that consisting of all things) were made public reality—Yes, sacrificed we were and the sacred pigeons' ears tingled to hear our gasps. (ADVANCING TO THE PAST "HELL" SURFACE AND DEEP THOUGHTS OF JAIL). In jails all over the world mountains of waste crap oozes on concrete floors, sweat from fallen men trickles from their hands and these beads of life shine the bars, reflect a human face before he leaves and trudges back to another spot, no so sad, not so gay—just a place called destination in such a shrunken world. For your cage has limitations—you know them in a day, maybe hours considering your individual complexes. Laughing men having fun seems old here, children, skies, horizons, hills, these values increase as a minute's value becomes your cell and these hours of minutes heat your body and work you unmercifully (poems rage wildly DREAMING THE PAST HELL) and you think your lines and believe them, your memory retracts before the pigeons landed and what would you should or shouldn't have done appears in minds for escape. But the door is shut, and you slam into it trying to defy the gates of time but always too late. This gate is closed, never to be open again. (Never try this door unless you are a lover of endless torment)—I speak to myself, of course, for minds everywhere are different and some agree just to be agreeing and some rebel just to be rebelling, but all are individual even though thoughts appear as twins.-- Not so in essence, in essence is purity. Wandering in that land, you never expect to visit, I've always wondered what it would be like to get busted and now I know. Stop wondering, you fool, you'll have plenty of time to know even more. I didn't even have my shoes on—yeah there I was, busted barefooted. He fits the part, I bet they said, and JB with his beard and Terry talking fast looking, thinking and realizing, to no avail. He fits too and we all fit; we all were in our places. Carry on, carry on, keep thinking, now I think all that hurts and I don't care. It's all so insane, maybe because I'm going that way. The morning sun keeps rising and grows more heated with the debates—the morning. So I walk a short stroll to the long room where we ate earlier and to seek relief from the heat from forty men and exposed windows from one sun, a sun I once loved for its natural beauty and the color it cast at dawn and later when it sinks on another world, and I could see the edge dip to darkness, the span it left behind I loved, every day was a new world, every day held a promise of new awareness. Is it worth it now? All I want is oblivion, nothing more, complete silence, complete unawareness, complete simplicity of nothingness to roam through my being and forget to care, forget to understand, to quit seeking values higher than the grave we live in. I reached to stop his vision, to retreat this vomiting of a reeling mind. It seems too late now. I want to see through darkened eyes eternity, death's eternity. I argue for life's side, I hold and shake till I listen, slap myself and say, listen!, listen! Shut up!! Time is your escape, wait till you see the sun setting just for you, pick a flower and see its colors with new eyes. Man understands limits, earthquakes, bombs, and stop—signs. So much more is there. Oh, when will it end? It ends only in your mind, two months, three months. Your values will stand ever brighter by this experience. I HANG LIMPLY FROM THE CAGER BARS AND CRY SOFTLY NOT WANTING TO BE SEEN. FINALLY, SOMEHOW I FIND STRENGTH SOMEWHERE TO BREATHE DEEPLY AND STOP THINKING ABOUT ANYTHING FOR OR AGAINST ANY. I FIND SLEEP FINALLY, NO DREAMS, NO NOTHING, JUST PEACEFUL SLEEP THROUGH ALL THE SWEAT AND MUMBLING. LIFE WON THIS TIME, BUT I KNOW SECLUSION FROM FREEDOM WILL WIN A MENTAL DEATH IF HELD TOO LONG.

THE CONCLUSION OF THE SECLUSION

The morning sun rises slowly with essence as its name, like Satan himself, he bears down—rays droop in like benefits from hell—cordial openings for boiling water. I soak in heated swirls only the devil could have stirred so swiftly. Every breath proceeds thoughts would in gloom, physical and mental yokes all harnessed in the seclusion of this cage I live. (IN 1953 THE SPIRIT OF GOD DREW ME OUT OF THE PEW), God drew me out of the pew, into the aisle and down to accept my Lord's salvation. I don't remember what Rev. Lunsford said, but I'll never forget the joy of that small, small boy. I received my crown, salvation's prize, but in the years to come, I believed a lie. I received my crown, but refused the sword that fights right and all sin abhors. THE WORD OF GOD and THE HOLY GHOST, the very things I needed most, I laid aside, then bore the cost. It wasn't long and I forgot His name and only remembered when it was used in vain. My teenage years had come and gone that night the man said "Here's the phone, one call is all you get." 1966 was a dreadful year, void of joy, void of cheer. To view my life was hard to bear—my parents cried and the world denied any hope for such a boy. One night I wrote the words I quoted first and cried inside from bitter thirst, for the Word of God and the Holy Ghost. After 13 years in Babylon, I kneel'd down low beneath the load of wild life oats which I had sown, and on my knees I said, "Oh, please, Please, dear Lord, take me home." God heard that prayer from this lost sheep and began to guide my stumbling feet. How he did it I'll never know, but I'll never forget there on that road, that night I stumbled in form Babylon. Jerusalem's lights were as the floods of joy that I once knew as a small boy, so many years ago. God brought me back from hell on earth to share His word through the Holy Ghost, and though I live by his abundant grace, and behold all joy in Jesus' face—and though my foot's on solid ground and my eyes look up and never down—still the past of hell on earth, yet lives within the ones I hurt—

CHRIST'S SALVATION AS IT BEGINS, SHOULD CONTINUE ON TILL THE VICTORIES END, BUT WITHOUT GOD'S WORD AND THE HOLY GHOST-- WELL, LOOK WHAT HAPPENED TO ME DOWN THE ROAD TO BABYLON.

Lord, It Ain't So Bad

By David P. Carlson

Weeds and Vines and trees a-dying, carefully I unearth
their remains—balling and crying, hurting and lying.
Some people think living and dying is just the same—
but I've found a new refrain—
When I see dark, I see the Light;
When I see gray, I turn and pray and I say, "Lord, it
ain't so bad, no it ain't so bad"--carefully I unearth the
remains. Four score and ten from the beginning to end,
"Lord, it ain't so bad";
knowledge creeps in along the ground—hopes and
hobbies further down—no strength to strike the
crusted soil, only shadows in the brain remain to
exclaim, "Lord, it ain't so bad, no it ain't so bad".
How far is the horizon? How high the mountain peaks
they're on? How deep must we dredge to find the
strength to search among the remains, careful not to
disturb the resting place of something more than
memories past; and once again, " Lord it ain't so bad,
no, it ain't so bad".

Machiavellian

by David P. Carlson

While diligently and furiously depending on the continual onslaught of the slaughtering of
helpless citizens, these world-class shroud-cladded, shadow-faced aristocrats join together to
count the days when they might cunningly escalate those measly murdered few to a
thousand-thousand, all to merge on time to be enshrined for a mere donation of their
sacrificially staged parading on those holy grounds of a multitude of plasma screens for
propaganda's sake, to solidify for all of this their common goal to control the frightened,
afraid and terrified.

Headlines scream the pain of the slain today in Bible study, children slaughtered while at
play, twelve more tragically have been gunned down in their own home town's resting
place, their local majestic movie house complex arcades—some beheaded in plain sight, in
perfect view on the evening news—others suffering, laying wounded behind the walls of
our nation's malls or super grand sports arenas, bowling alleys and maybe even nursing
homes.

What is it that brings to this regimen of men (or just a simple ordinary soul) such joy to kill
and maim his fellow man? Could it be as simple as a sub—or conscious plan to be a world-
famous celebrity, to be flagged by a rag-tag professor, doctor, governmental or clinical
physiological team who loves to write about such things—such as the criminal politically
challenged sociopaths, and how their minds derive their train of thought down those broken
tracks so soon to be detailed on some holy grail, so then to eventually be deemed insanely
zealous of what they believe to be a holy tenet of some supreme life form, being Allah,
Buddha, maybe Socrates or the Dalai Lama, and then to be analyzed, personified and
finally understood to be the product of their own schizophrenic mental quest to reach that
emblematic emboldened status of supreme martyrdom;

Now this highly educated examining team just simply notes him or them to have contracted
a highly contagious social disease easily eradicated by a wholesome dose of therapy: Now
about this their convoluted grand desire for ethnic cleansing of the human race, well that, of
course, was brought about by Mom and Dad, or someone else they depended on that sadly
let them down, or maybe it's this nation's Laws and Rights he or they love to trample on.

(over)

48

Nevertheless they seem to all agree, "It's really just our educated guess". I guess that's why it will take so long to scotch their rumors of the impending annihilation of Christendom.

Now because of all this chaos we all take part for all can see how common sense can spark a super-sonic spending spree for buried bunkers, just the place to store the family's picture album, Gatling guns, rocket launchers and machetes: then up we go to the great outdoors to take a tour through the fields of orange, peach and apple trees, there to pick a few for a tasty snack while the kids and neighbors scurry far and wide to find some rocks and bricks to help build the moat around their castle's towering walls, sturdily built over six feet thick, so there to hide and house their tanks and trucks abundantly stocked with poison gas and booby traps, just in case they might run across some of those roving bands of zombies, Nazis, or gypsy clans who may decide to invade the land.

But with all of this, our well-planned defense, all is never really ever well, for you can always tell with a single glance the face behind the mask, Beelzebub, the Antichrist, there to proclaim a truce to take us all away to that promised land to place a noose around our necks, and there to be introduced to his Sharia lawlessness.

Truth is, "the soul that sinneth shall surely die," physically and that highly debated spiritual side. Now all of this life on earth has stirred mankind so that he has reached his final apogee, so much farther away from that heavenly bond than could ever have been imagined, others so near to that heavenly perigee, better known as that moment shown as when God lets you know you're not alone, so near you'll hear him whisper "Welcome home, be of good cheer, I have overcome this world's shrouded, shadow-faced aristocrats whose common goal is to control with hate (their favorite tool), the terrified and alone. But, when I come sayeth the Lord, they will be the ones to cringe in fear behind their closet doors—once again my chosen friends, my begotten ones—fear not, we all will overcome by enduring to THE END.

Matador, Picadores, and the Bull--El Picayune

By David P. Carlson

Circling; taunting the mysterious picayune creature upon the ground El Picador plots another painful jab. From on high, astride his prancing beast, el picador feels compelled to take the call on his red and yellow vibrating cell of a phone. What a time to be disturbed when life and death are on the line. (No pun intended). Now peering over his tree trunk boarded barricade El Matador prepares for his dramatic entrance dance. After a little pirouette he stumbles into the bull's domain to claim the life of El Picayune, the sacrifice for a cheering few. Oddly enough, the bull seems calm as El Matador scrambles around to find his sword, his cape and one tennis shoe. Finally when all his paraphernalia has been returned from the grand arena's "lost and found" he again emerges from the wings, this time half dressed with sword in hand and a silly grin to attack that beast in a fit of rage; then cries "I'll kill your hide even if it be with my own bare hands!!", but just in time the bull, he steps aside and gores El Matty in both hip and side, and on top of that, he tore his pants. That's when Matty screamed out for Picador and his boys and said, "you need to stab this bull a few more times if I'm gonna do the crime." Well, when that didn't work out so good, old Matty just pulled out his gun and shot that bull, then went his way to fight again another day.

Well, the moral or the lesson I'm guessin' is, if you're gonna fight the Devil and his crowd on his own turf, don't wait till he pulls a gun; just gore him where it will do some good; then take his sword and his cape, and as he turns and limps away call him Picayune Paltry, or with an old Webster's English definition it might be better said--"Oh, ye of little worth!!"

Monastic Wind—Inane Branches

By David P. Carlson

Green and thin now equates to trembling lusts of chlorophylling
gel within the veins of leaves from their long extended stems and
branches. The relentless gusts of winter's breath bends then twists
till all seems lost, all is tossed from side to side till the wind
collides, buckles and then subsides again. Motionless, the limbs
silently weep and groan, as the tear-like sap flows from those
countless leaves and splintered twigs they once caressed (but now
sadly are bereaved) as their seed-rich stems ,all now strewn and
broken upon the ground, then seized by God, there to be whisked
away by another late December breeze.

The wind; your friend or foe? Oh, but for sure a force to be
reckoned with—Consult the forest, consult the Lake and all that
is therein. Death and Life both consort to move ahead—so march
they do in one accord, in lock and step their steady stride; so they
do and carry on in unison until they both receive the call, the
commander's loud resounding cry "Halt!, stand at ease,
now kindly step aside."

Now stiff and straight the limbs of death and life stand as one
shivering there in the airless damp dark abyss. With a blustery
gush, the wind picks up again to strive alive; again to carry them
to their timeless quest to understand the power of the wind—but
without the air life and death remain secure. As the wind subsides
the serenity of it all sets them both adrift.

(over)

The wind, the force in every death, in every life merely withdraws those cloistered chlorophyll-filled stems of life from deep within man's futile attempts to show respect. Finally in their last of days the limbs can only gently sway and reluctantly break away. No more a place for tears to form and freeze, glistening as they dangle there upon the branch of another winter day—the wind simply grins, then silently slips away, leaves his monasterial cloist-er to grieve again another day.

Monastically, this cloistered wind miraculously transposes nature's natural metamorphosis while swirling down to change in form – oh so greatly now—flash the lightning—and as the thunder trumpets his grand eternal transformation he reaches out clutching all within his path amidst the clouds aloft, then spiraling low to grasp the prey to control the swaying motions of another set of inanimate branches along the way.

There are more than two, maybe more some summer days in which the wind whips the limbs of your ever-growing contemplations. Some of you thank the storm for controversies, some take the blunt of the hurricane that rip your young and fragile saplings to the ground. Howling or gently flowing this carousel-like wind is forever in control of our every goings and all of our abatings. But in the ever-looming end of life's seasons, life will spring forth her light to at last reveal the loving face of God, and there again the force of life, his ever present Wind.

Never Ending Rain

By David P. Carlson

Among the clouds the moisture hides within those towering
chambered walls, content to ride the rising heat to meet the cold
and frigid air aloft, to spawn therein the warmth wherein she
hibernates--while on earth her friends, the trees, the plants, the
grass all gather there to germinate, waiting patiently for the
rumbling thunder behind the flash of lightening strikes to flush
the sky of her abundant rain on those starless and windy nights.

As drops of rain, each tear in life is loosed on high to fall, then
grace the sky with the scented incense essence of a human kind of
kindness, a trait once held sublime; destined tears (that plunge as
streaks to meet the earth on those cloudy sunless days), spill their
lives for that hope that man, that wife and child may come to
realize the price of love; so that they might sup, then rise to grow
up tall, to shed the pain of their obdurate and fruitless lives.

So now, as their sublimeness has been regained they lift up their
leaves as an evening shower sprays the soil with early mourning-
drops as tears, to once again regerminate, then cultivate a new
genetic strain to reign and rhyme with the God who created the
human soul and mind – a soul designed to be revived by
humankind, another kind of sacrifice that leads to harvest time
by his never-ending rain.

Ordinary Angle

By David P. Carlson

"What can you spare my brother?" breathed the aged prophet to the scribe. I'll tithe a farthing and a mite, never mind the cost; but mind you, sir, all the silver and all the gold can ne'er repair nor soothe the pain contained within this tomb of hopes assumed as doomed, better known as mediocrities.

As the stench of despair is masked with a hint of mint and a dash of authenticity, the aroma slightly impairs his sarcastic mood, but still inspires the imprisoned scribe to print with feathered pen his questions upon the wall—Am I without or am I within this united state of mediocre; am I just another shell upon the sand in a land long forgotten? Is this my day to be crowned with eternal anonymity, now verging on the first stages of narcolepsy;

"Really?" It may sound silly or a bit insane to quibble about my quest in life, to seek a higher plain, to labor in this sea of sand; but tell me, sir, from where you stand outside this tomb, where have I gone astray or shall I begin again another day?

Once again breathed the prophet to the scribe, "What can you spare that you might find or what portion will you be willing to cosign; surely more than a farthing or a mite. Now, just pay your tithes, repent and pray, then weigh your wages each and every day. Live for God who sent His Son and know that nothing is ever deemed mediocre if God receives from you at least his ten percent and, maybe, just a little over.

Pity

By David P. Carlson

A graveyard empty. A man leans and picks a
flower for no one but himself; His name is pity—
His heart has no soul—He murmurs a lonely song
he memorized because he felt it was to him—
He knows nothing of what he does—He only
thinks, "if it were only like that I could be happy"-
He talks to lonely people—He speaks aloud to
empty rooms thinking someday he'll find someone
to listen.
He writes a sad tale, then feels he's failed to
describe himself very well—
What will happen to a man like this? Find his
way, find his heart? Who will listen when all is
said? Only no one. Only hell.

Salvation's Happy Days
By David P. Carlson

Saints glide with me across blue-grey skies—
Pink roses garnish my hair as the wind ruffles the
bellowing clouds—
I dance in horizons filled with hope.
Eyes reflect the glorious sight—
I reach for life with outstretched arms.
I behold sights fading, flicking deep upon my
smiling face—
The branch of life sways in godly breaths—
Tender emotions sink from within starlit skies—
Darkness melts around me—
I fade into it another night, looking forward to
another day and another night to kneel and pray.

Soul Searchers

By David P. Carlson

The truth spoken in corridors of lines, blended in the
longing of life, now kneel dented by the pressures of a
wondering mind, speckled with the experience of time,
of situations so long forgotten but still left suspended
in the infancy of truth, or what seemed truthful.
To me sainted beliefs span as a shadow of a wondering
mind on landscapes of purity.
With this we breed years of gasping decisions.
I need the belief that someone has sometime needed one
blissful minute wrapped in one word spoken from the
soul.

Summer Rain
By David P. Carlson

A black framed screen again holds my portrait—
through it I see the violence of nature's emotions;
flashing anger erupts.
The beauty I once found erupts—the beauty I once
found, (cascading in all its glory, seasoned glory)
chills not one fiber in me.
There held in dark reverence, my life—rain drops
barely heard, raindrops hang the trees with tears—
air rests silently—I hear my heart like distant
thunder—I find nature's violence within me—
My eyes flash surrender to summer rain.

The Arrow, the Archer, the Bow and String

By David P. Carlson

The bow layered with gopher, shittim wood and cedar, stained and
polished, shaped by time even before it started. Such a grand
transformation of an array of past transactions; now with bow in tack
the master archer begins to weave but a single strand of linen, twined
with silk, woven without a seam, yet so thin and common as a single,
simple ordinary string; he'll stretch it out to fit the bow when bent, now
content to be the finial cord, he'll secure it tight and fast to the last belay,
there to withstand the constant strain, oh so taut between the to-and-fro
of the alpha and omega's poles.

Now with bow in hand the master archer needs but one more precious
item to be found and spent, a quiver full of only one straight and narrow
armor-piercing arrow. This arrow now fit and feathered, now set and
glued has but one more step to be tried and then approved, to be bound up
tight, certified to be accounted sublimely worthy to be the shaft of life, to
be laid upon the master's bow.

With string set tight within the arrow's hasp the mighty archer draws
back his bow, and with prey in sight (with one more belated breath) he lets
the arrow go. You might say at that moment there in time, their was a
greatly strained relationship between the archer, arrow string and bow.
Rapprochement is the word I have in mind which simply means to me, a
restoration of a once strained, then broken eternal tie with all mankind;
now thanks be to God (the master archer) for the arrow lent, prepared for
the flight, to forgive, so now to find its mark upon the heart of all the
lives since time was derived. Such is our life we seek each day upon the
bow and string, an arrow to be let go.

The Camel and the Fox

By David P. Carlson

The camel and the fox, a peculiar pair; friends for life, compelled to
share their lives within the lion's lair. Computers sing a constant
stream of information; but soon the camel shows his extremely
strained and futile frustrations—"If only I were sly and quick, so as
to note what keys to click, I'd order up a batch of tricks to trap that
old fox, then save his tail to hang around my neck for my first trip to
the "Casino Sands" there in Nevada's land. Now with some luck, I'd
win the cup, and then when I'd cashed in I'd pay the price and bisect
these humps (though filled with life and nourishment) and trade
them in for a trip to the Promised Land, in the land of the midnight
sun. Now on my sleigh of six-foot wide, I'd wave goodbye to the
Land of Sand and that old fox and his sarcastic grin. Now he would
be the one with the lonesome gaze, left to trod the sand without a
tail to sway from side to side. I would wish him luck, but as it is,
I'll retain my humps and just be me; that's just life you see--or do we;
Ya know that old fox we desire to deceive just could be you and me
from time to time, a dueling set of personalities. That old Camel, he
seems slow ya know, kinda saunters around and feeds on grass and,
"Hey!", he's just trying to get along. But that old fox; he's rude at
times, his temper's quick and sometimes he's out of line. So let's just
crank it back a bit and start this poem once again. Now for Mr.
Camel and Mr. Fox to get along its gonna take a little time and a lot
of help from two of man's best friends; Father God and his Son—the
Word and the Chance they both get born again.

The Countess and the Beast

By David P. Carlson

Searching secretly through the compost-destined

Mounds of political turmoil is the Mind-Beast,

Patented and protected by the countless conspirators,

All courting the same Countess of Courtesy,

Veiled in her transparent gown,

Naked and exposed to her own opaque arrogance

That gropes through her endless array of deceptive attires—

"Politically correct" yet completely disconnected from

All her common interests that once was "Life and Liberty",

And now she comfortably lies in the lap of all her comforters

While frolicking in the mire of her deceptiveness—

This Mind-Beast, Father to all her compulsions,

Now truly is perfidy and totally incoherent to the masses.

His mind-set is totally dedicated to his objectives

(over)

And now to us all is obviously oblique to all his surroundings
Of smoking mirrors and shouting orators.
Now hand-in-hand the Countess and the Beast in lockstep
Precision march down this stained-glass road
Where eternity's light will never shine,
Politically correct in every way,
But in his house his mirrors have forever denied his kind,
For never a reflection can ere be seen,
Because of his own opaque-crusted mind.
The Countess and the Beast now need another site
To speak their wedding vows,
Where eyes and ears are mute and blind,
Where Hate and Death can truly rhyme
Outside the sight of Truth and Love—
Transparency of another kind can only wait
By Faith, on the Other Side.

The Dark Ages

By David P. Carlson

Behind thine eyes lies a brain—complicated and confused—

Through precious sight we breed pure-bred knowledge of our surroundings to this mind-beast—pollened and spermed by every fathering moment.

Dry brown limbs crackle, crack silently as puppets for silent winds.

Beetles, Crickets, all small crawling things scurry as men beneath sequoia forests.

Their world of living phenomena is as our own. The Dark Ages in miniature is their environment and truly must be their own.

A scream, a shout, rumbling motors, wailing whistles, blasts from guns, all are but echoes from the human world above.

Brisk winds—forest's noises, the swish and crash of falling dying limbs are as the beginning, the Dark Ages.

Night descends with the passing light—winds clutch—hold still clear nights—upon dark-blue velvet skies sparkle lights of years before. Dark-green sprouts of emerging youth hang face-down in absents of the wind.

Then a rumble in the heavens—a flash of light turns green emerging youth—a gust of moist autumn rain shines her surface—propels her motions with stormy violence.

Young green grass sprouts dance with new emotions, whips in autumn's breath, damp with season's tears—

Beside emerging youth, the old and dying and the dead. Storm clouds move, then chatter in the distance—

A full moon looms in hazy patterns behind the basking clouds—

A barking dog barks the night into silence, leaves a green grass sprout crying tears upon a dark-brown grave, in miniature even prayed.

The Gray Day
By David P. Carlson

Through misty fog waters, unshined space, the
appearance of gray is conceived without power of
thought and reasoning.
The gray of a dawnless day flows into the cavities of
the mind like hot lead into its mold.
But why is such a flow standard to more than half?
Cannot it be conceived as in between bliss from dark
and brilliance,
A peaceful inheritance of blended thoughts cradled in
the cool damp rival of dominant colors.
So it is for me.

The Jasmine of the Night

Cestrum nocturnum

Cestrum nocturnum (common names include **night-blooming jasmine**, **night-blooming cestrum**, **lady of the night**, **queen of the night**, **night-blooming jessamine**, and **Hāsnūhānā** (Bengali: is a species of cestrum in the plant family Solanaceae (the potato family). It is native to the West Indies but naturalized in South Asia.

Night-blooming jasmine is an evergreen woody shrub growing to 4 meters (13 ft) tall. The leaves are simple, narrow lanceolate, 6–20 centimeters (2.4–7.9 in) long and 2–4.5 centimeters (0.79–1.77 in) broad, smooth and glossy, with an entire margin. The flowers are greenish-white, with a slender tubular corolla 2–2.5 centimeters (0.79–0.98 in) long with five acute lobes, 10–13 millimeters (0.39–0.51 in) diameter when open at night, and are produced in cymose inflorescences. A powerful, sweet perfume is released at night. The fruit is a berry 10 millimeters (0.39 in) long by 5 millimeters (0.20 in) diameter, the color of an aubergine. There is also a variety with yellowish flowers. There are mixed reports regarding the toxicity of foliage and fruit.

The Jasmine of the Night

By David P. Carlson

The moon arrives in its iron cage, the lock is snapped, then thrust aside. This nocturnal mother-of-pearl breaks through the silence of the night to emerge from behind that rainforest's golden doors; a time to shine in this place where truth and lies collide, to blossom once again by the power of her moonlight hour, this jasmine of the night.

The Jasmine of the Night

By David P. Carlson

The moon arrives in its iron cage, the lock is snapped, then thrust aside. This nocturnal mother-of-pearl breaks through the silence of the night to emerge from behind that rainforest's golden doors; a time to shine in this place where truth and lies collide, to blossom once again by the power of her moonlight hour, this jasmine of the night.

A perfect place for this poem to have found its end, but still this cestrum nocturnum flower has scarce but one night, one life to unfold her greenish paragon of inflorescence beauty from deep within; then sadly destined there to fade and shrivel, as to once again succumb to the brilliance of God's relentless sun, to evaporate her sweet perfumed fragranced dew from up off her long solicitous and solemn leaves for another continual ending of her nocturnal space of grace, so marked by a quick retreat into her hibernated, reclusive state, so forlorn.

Now surging through her withering stems and blossoms, there still flows a divine desire from God alone, a cherished goal to bare her soul before a greater light, there to display her truth, to deny the lie that life and death can co-exist within the gloom of this dark abyss we call the night, there beneath the fog of this diminished moonlight glow—this lesser light so caged and locked can only now recant his claim on the jasmine families name, "Solanaceae"—for now to his chagrin this flower blossoms only for one greater light within, the one that grants to her the right to live and bloom once again, in a land where there is no night.

So is the promised hope for the jasmine of the night, to forgive, then bloom and blossom within the sight of the living God, never to have her beauty hid, but forever displayed, arranged and named by God himself as his sweetly savored bouquet delight, the now transformed, "Jasmine of the Light".

The Parachute

By David P. Carlson

We live in times of war on distant shores, yet war is all around us;
The currents of life swirl in the pools of our own glass-cast
aquariums as the signs of the times flicker upon the walls and
screens before our eyes, then die to dreams in our dark unconscious
hours.

Death and Greed (spawned by transparent seeds, spilt by ancient
Cain and his descendants) beckons us from the blackened coals of
burned out trees in the deep beyond below, "Proceed, Proceed"—

Is this the cliff time has prepared for all mankind? Over and
down, through such a massive cloud of emptiness, we need not
fear to go. If only we could procure a handy parachute, to then
regain control of life's destined plans to purge our precious
atmosphere of the air we share; then, and only then, can we gently
settle down without a war to mar the ground,
our final resting place.

That parachute, of course, is Christ, who beckons us with His
loving voice, "Proceed, Proceed"; rest in peace with Me—
"For without Me, you can do nothing."

The Turtle and the Skunk

By David P. Carlson

Weird from here within this cave I bravely huddle in—I mean the light, the way it streams in, then flickers upon this maze of darkened corners, then jerks, then dances across the floor, then seems to disappear up and down through those cavern's corridors, then once again the darkness reaches in to close the door, thus sets me free to confront the sounds of alley cats, mice and rats clawing through a plethora of tin trash cans full of discarded foods and toys—Like music to my ears, this symphony of disconcerting abstracts all colliding, then come tumbling in like glass on pots and pans to one colossal crescendo before the end—Just another day within this turtle shell, my cardboard hell—oh well—Hey, what's that scratching on my shell, pray tell—oh, yeah, my friend, the skunk; he visits me from time to time to remind me there's another world out there—yeah, the one I fled in 2012—that's why I've come to this alley home to where I have now resigned to forever dwell—So now my goal is to escape from that old skunk I call my oracle or reality: I feel compelled to yell—"Hey, mate, what's going on out there?"—slowly I may, as turtles may someday, emerge from this cardboard box to again befriend that old skunk. (You may prefer to infer he should be addressed as my over-rated sanity).

(OVER)

It would be nice to shed this shell and walk upright again,
but then the question that will still arise is, "Why?"
But then the answer came, to my surprise, that old skunk was in
disguise. His true identity was the angle of the truth, void of lies
and vain deceit. The stench I smelled was not the skunk, but was
all those lies I'd buried there deep within those caverns beneath
this cranium shell I call my mind, that say there is no hell, no
heavenly paradise in which to dwell—no earthly test that we
must pass to overcome to hear God say, "Well done, my son, enter
in."—The only reality I once embraced was my own oblivious
state that denied the truth there within my laminated cardboard
case—now if I may, I do repent and shed this shell of hate for a
crown of life and two good wings to fly above this earthen pond
up to the gate where heaven waits to give a hug and welcome in,
both the turtle and the skunk.

Two Roses and a Music Box

By David P. Carlson

(Christ's prayer and flowers—
God's chimes in times of trouble)

Two roses and a music box, two hearts one simple song.
I pray, my dear, that your unborn tears will never be shed
alone; but if someday as roses may, you lose some petals in a
summer storm, then take these words or these chimes or this
heart of mine and shine a rainbow through your tears;

The day in the life of a rainbow bright, how brief the light
of her life. The memory of her gaze on that bright but rainy
day, to me will be a sea of green and gold, so as the light
from the dawn bends shadows along the pathways of your
mind, let the green and the gold beneath the rainbow's bow
be the treasure of your soul—so take these words or these
chimes or this heart of mine and shine a rainbow through
your tears.

Vertigo—the Illusion of Euphoria

(The family reunion of Vertigo, Euphoria Grandeur and Illusion with Family Friend, Johnny Pride—The Adventure)

By David P. Carlson

Back flip into the icy blue, his tanks filled up to the brim by a slight of hand, a massive dose of vertigo. Tumbling down to what his mind thinks is up, he goes higher into the depths below, there to swim in the illusion that sharks and fools are his potential friends with whom he prefers to roam—but truth can plainly see he swims along alone. Now sinking into the abyss (that he mistakenly viewed as the path to abysmal blessedness) he sees emerging from beneath the grandeur mountain peaks his manifesto request, written and approved, his task assigned for him to climb the icy slopes of Mt. Illusion to the grandeur that he seeks.

Just in time, slithering up from the heights below his beautiful sea-green creature friend, Queen Euporia. On her back he'll hitch a ride to the base camp on the other side of Mt. Grandeur, and there he'll prepare to climb. He'll pack a meager lunch of tasty crumbs and don his wares with camel humps (another tank of what he thinks is air) and then from there he'll scale those daunting peaks below.

There he'll scroll there on that sandbar shoal "My NAME is Johnny Pride" and on this peak I'll stake my claim to be the greatest orator and adventurer ALIVE: but then to his dismay he sees the arrogance in his twisted LIE—had spelled it wrong,--and now etched in stone his claim to fame now begins to erode, then to wash away from the sandstone shallows of his brain, the residue of vertigo. As an ocean surge he rises up once more to say—my name is now Johnny Shame, and by my erratic acts I do deduce my best excuse is my highly impaired equilibrium. Exhausted, confused, and bruised; now sprawled there flat upon his back he finally clearly sees the illusion of euphoria has no grandeur to attract—with one last gasp he finds his breath, then reaches up to grasp the love and mercy in God's hands, but this time without his gloves. Now Grace and Faith soar as one to restore his will to breathe and live again firmly upon his raft above. From there he'll journey up to the shore do dine with God, sip from the cup of Life and Love with Him forevermore. The grandeur man has been looking for at last, alas the perfect metaphor has now made clear, there is no vertigo with God; with God the way is always UP, his directions always SURE.--AMEN

Virginia Lester Bochler Young

By David P. Carlson

The woman be my mother—Virginia Lester
Bochler Young—her past I know of none—her
voice a distant hum. Her face a ghostly place
within my mind-- Virginia Lester Bochler Young.
Twenty-five years and eight months ago, I know I
hurt her some. She gave life, yes, Lester's wife—
Virginia Lester Bochler Young.
Was it rainging the night I was born, Mother?
Was lightening striking, Mother? The night I was
born, was the wind howling down the streets there
in Dearborn town, the night I was born?
Was Lester waiving in the hospital hall, Mother?
Was he sitting down or doing the town—and
wishing I were dead? How I must have burdened
you that cold and dreary night Mother.
Well, as of this day, I've wedded twice and not
one child was born to me—for a child to me would
be like a child in Virginia's arms—a seed you
planted well—Virginia Lester Bochler Young.

Vision

By David P. Carlson

Is man is a mere version of the immaculate, eidetic creator, even endowed with certain idiosyncrasies so as to be enjoined within the incarnation of goodness yet to have an innate trait of evil,—thus among us the perverted versions, all yet to be converted?

Can a child be simply a product of genetic biological grafting in that the mere essence of such a literary idiomatic joining (or better said "God-sent") of these three separate entities, "sequence of places", "time", and "events" simply to be viewed as inane or even mundane occurrences, designed to populate the planet?

Flash a momentary flickering upon the screen that fluctuates, so to be deemed by man weather to be sane or insane. The man though nattily is mainly a multi-functional, yet mostly a singularly focused species bent on dominating one and only one sphere of a self-proclaimed characteristic, that of continual conjecture.

Now considering the isthmus between man and God, from vision to version, now set a course, now not so blaringly ennui, but with your heart in hand transcend and spin, careen across those raging streams and roaring rivers,-- now join as one with both boat and rider, crashing through those foaming rapids, smashing, lurching, frantically searching, groping, clawing to grab those dangling vines and drooping limbs from that rock embedded bank, so then to subdue the relentlessness of this marching torrent, raging toward the impending waterfall of death, a fate of life's eternal end.

(over)

Oh, but remarkably sir, this master Olympic mariner of sorts, bravely plunges headlong in with a fearless grin to swim upstream against the tide, to then emerge with anchor dangling from his side to greet the cheers of admiring fans he is now so rightly been endeared.

That manly version, now reclines, convalescing in the dark regions and reservoirs of his mind. Now coveting what he believes himself to be, that total package, the enigma man in combat mode, extinguishing all of life's istical infernos of fears from within his mind, but unknowingly he has been graphically impaled before a body of his peers; but amazingly he is still convinced there upon his cot of the veracity of his noble plight—but then the vision flickers once again upon the screen; time relents, colors fade as the isthmus between the vision and the version experiences a devastating, crippling and total collapse——so of course the vision of his creation sadly comes to rest at the conclusion of his course. No need to revise another profound infusion of another perverted version——

That which comes from the original is an original in itself——but that which is perverted becomes a version——not the vision of the Creator.

Waiting in the Wings of the Final Hour: Chimera, Countess of Terror

By David P. Carlson

Chimera awakened—this aristocracy-type of goat of sorts,
snake-tailed, fire-breathing female, terror-breeding sociopath,
far more than a mythical monster of Greek mythology—
making up her face to deceive the minds of all mankind,
while all the while this nation's pride has gone so sadly far
astray, striding tirelessly over the edge of time's most awaited
sacrosanctic hour, "The end of time", where ticks are replaced
with judgments and tocks by multitudes of regrets, all
slipping over the ledge into those crosswinds of cosmic space
without limits, where limits are forever lost in an unlimited
span of ornately painted vermillion sails, all so furiously
driven by those solar winds of God's universal condemnation
of Chimera's recreant fallen angels.
These antediluvian faces of past and present counters with
cursings, sucking in with every breath her venom to then be
injected into the protoplasm of demented men.
Chimera, this lioness of evil, this didactical professor of
recalcitrance, her tail of ruby-studded sins, all engulfed by her
vomiting flames within the solar plexus of men, always to be
just one click away from many ephemerally inserted moments
of "pshaw", then left to enjoy her rewards for wickedness
from within the realm of this nation's laws without reproach
from this nation's moral codes of acronymic words, so
disguised that no one can assume what's right or wrong, only
what seems able to conform to fill that empty gloom, surely
right for at least one afternoon.

(over)

Chimera, the worlds' so-called last hope for an antidote to cure what she calls Christendom's prevaricated hope for divine immortality. So now there for all to embrace, a few alphabetically arranged collections of Chimer's acrimonious thoughts, all contrived within the mind of who else, this anti-Christian caped-crusader, now waiting for her final fate, the prophetic conformation for a time no longer allowed to procrastinate or sit and ponder, now only silence just before that inviolable hour where once again Chimera hears, "The mysteries of God has been forever finished", thus saith the seventh angel of Revelation, Ten-six and seven.

Wind—

By David P. Carlson

The wind, the force in every death, in every life merely withdraws
those cloistered chlorophyll-filled stems of life from deep within
man's futile attempts to show respect. Finally in their last of
days the limbs can only gently sway and reluctantly break away.
No more a place for tears to form and freeze, glistening as they
dangle there upon the branch of another winter day—the wind
simply grins, then silently slips away, leaves his monasterial
cloist-er to grieve again another day.

Monastically, this cloistered wind miraculously transposes
nature's natural metamorphosis while swirling down to change in
form – oh so greatly now—flash the lightning—and as the
thunder trumpets his grand eternal transformation he reaches out
clutching all within his path amidst the clouds aloft, then
spiraling low to grasp the prey to control the swaying motions of
another set of inanimate branches along the way.

There are more than two, maybe more some summer days in which
the wind whips the limbs of your ever-growing contemplations.
Some of you thank the storm for controversies, some take the blunt
of the hurricane that rip your young and fragile saplings to the
ground. Howling or gently flowing this carousel-like wind is
forever in control of our every goings and all of our abatings. But
in the ever-looming end of life's seasons, life will spring forth her
light to at last reveal the loving face of God, and there again the
force of life, his ever present Wind.

Winter's Land

By David P. Carlson

At times love is beautiful—Love has many loves echoing in time;
beckoning to be had—

Souls filled with happy smiles, fade with winter's coming—

Green plagues empty rooms—Hope emerges, denies defeat—

Life stands clear through anxious waiting, then disfigures in
sundown shadows—

Summer flows – Fall fails – Spring brings new love – Winter
howls surrender—

Lives wither as cold love numbs—

Hearts take love from within our hallowed dreams—sitting;
facing winter nights, night winds beckon—

Rain drops hang your face with tears—Human drops on human
skin take your warmth—leaves you clutching winter's hand—
warmth a precious thing when winter comes.

So now, solicitously I stand in winter's robe, clutching warmth
where I can. I reach to feel the cold might wind, Tears on winter's
face I touch, Her sadness holds me, clutching warmth where she
can. I take her hand, I understand—her tears splash, then turn to
ice. A winter's night has found a friend.

Within Us
By David P. Carlson

Blue skies—Red skies—Tenderness;
Then love; Life darts within us—
Death kneels before us.
A sparrow fell yesterday—his lifeless form then turns
to ashes—His was a simple life—he was without sin.
He surely felt the pain of death—His death brought joy
to some small boy.
He was surely not a man!
Blue skies—Red skies
In heaven they felt the pain.

Youth Plight—Velvet Covered Antlers in the Snow

By David P. Carlson

Consequences, the grand order of judgment; consequences, the perfect reward for obedient children from a loving and understanding creator. Now surely, surly is this juvenile/man, there left behind among those shining pines of this winter's testing grounds, there to wear those diamond-studded colored buttons upon his velvet-covered manly antlers, so deeply buried in the snow. Truly a novice so perfectly denotes his stature, truly naïve, reflects the pattern of his wanderings through the snow and ice-covered shoals.

There stretched upon his bed of definitiveness among the shrubs, tangled weeds and dangling thatches, he ponders the worth of his life-long conclusions that daily guide his way to that manly state of maturity. Complicated is his journey among the vines of daily-invoked rhetorically-framed hypothetical questions followed by streams of rapid-infested rivers of equally intimidating, if not discriminating choices of answers, all echoing through those cerebral canyon chasms of rock granite cliffs, so secludedly entombed within his own sub-degrees of ice and snow, that minute clusters of painful blisters are soon formed, so divinely packed within his frozen stare that then he sees the void of his own last days and there as well, with his mind impaired by his crippling mental hypothermia, he contradicts his prior pleas of mercy and equality there beneath the frozen grass and leaves of reality. Curiously those little winter birds inspect those velvet-covered antlers in the snow, then chirp and sail away through those flying crystal specks of glass like ice as they go their way. Now to their dismay those lifeless antlers shake as though still attached to some living creature's face, eyes and nose.

Then slowly there he gathers strength to stand and face the sun's resplendent chromospheric glow——resurrection now unfolds for those velvet-covered antlers in the snow.

(over)

Such is our hope to avoid such tragic consequences of a youthful life not yet fully followed through. Such is the gorge between the young and old and rightly so, for Father God and man. So unveil the crimson velvet shroud from off those horns of God's eternal alter. The battle waits; no room for doubt, no time left to falter—with cloak in hand his youth unfurls this his velvet stained vermillion shroud, left to dangle in shredded strips, dripping blood to the snow below, exposed to all of this life's wildernesses of predatorial guests that pause, then quickly stand to see this massive stag receive his granted promise, his elegant crown of horns to rule the land, to fight and clash with all that might attempt to mount his throne, to trample down his well-deserved manly antlers held high above the melting snow.

Anthracite and Dexterous
A Horse and Buggy to Watch for at the Finish Line
By David P. Carlson

With dexterity shriveling and shredded youth enjoined within the stiffening order, this fragile man with his demurring spirit now dares to denounce their so-called premise of his predestinated, inevitable, soon demise, so contrived within the eyes of his accusers.

Slanted are those rolling hills of a man's last days, also those projected summits of each his aspirations, all then to be chronologically enhanced, judged to be enigmatic, then sent spiraling outward by those hostile blasts of distraught dissenters to the apogee of his life's-long goals of extended youth (a true superlative of abundant dexterity so desired by all mankind). This second wind, if you may, to ascend within the realm of his own intense desire to fly upon the wings of his antiquated antediluvian (yet far from obsolete) horse and buggy body— to ignite to his delight his love for life and something to look forward to in the last days of his anthracitical existence, though so intense the heat, so low the flame, so minute the smoke, all so designed to deny the complete unconspicuousness of it all.

Does this now sound as the sort of man that would resort to desperate gropings for cords within to secure a hand to hold or some convenient notch to clutch among those jagged rocks of insecurity? Now, I say, all of this I pray is to encourage his intentions to prevail beyond his allotted time before the eyes of his equally aged fellow-elders, to be reborn and then rebounded with new dexterity within his human mind's soulful core. Continually we shrivel and stiffen from life to death, then to be revived again by uncoquettish and decorous spirits in constant search for our diademed transcendent such known as the Giver of dexterous youth, the Alpha, the Omega, Jesus Christ

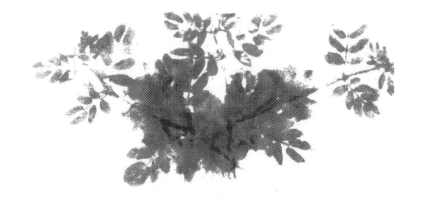

Fallen Leaves- Abandoned Branches
By David P. Carlson

Fallen Leaves- Abandoned Branches

By David P. Carlson

As this oak tree's limbs bend and sway in a late winter's blustery gust
of recollected memories (all born of yesterday's summer meditations) she
sheds her leaves like snow (or maybe like a serpent's skin upon the road
of multi-misconceptions) but leaves a few for early spring to cover those
untraveled lanes within her mind, even on the path to her hometown
back-yard patio, all sent tumbling silently down, thrumming along, all
agape, recalling to their dismay those recanted hollow promises of
joyous springtime escapades, all so imprudently scampering stealthily
out of view from there atop of this great oak's perch of an imperious,
impiously imbibed eidetically attained attitude, but still she sees and is
content to watch her leaves be trod afoot there beneath those dead and
dying wooden mazes, there to flip and sail through twigs and stems of
abandoned nests of doves, sparrows, bluebirds, and tiny wrens and
hummingbirds, finally down, pell-mellently resting on the forest's floor
below, all of this left to steer another metaphor to parallel its self
aversely into our lives upon the tangled branches of our lively forest's
cultures. How green and tender is the new-born leaf upon the stem?
How many years from spring to spring will come to pass before the
savage task of growing faithful to the command of a fresh commitment
to dedication. How many storms with lightening strikes can be endured
before the return of early spring to count the ones upon the soiled and
tattered truff of anonymity, then to hear the swish of man-made
brooms to sweep away those countless disconcerted lives into assorted
piles of resentful forms of repetitiousness—now from high above those
tangled branches (of what she so often termed her brambles) she sees the
hordes of stranded lives taken down by those winter winds of youthful
pride, all laid to rest in the notes of a mournful song on those solemn
summer nights of deep regrets among those pellucidict forest noises,

(over)

now to be whisked away before the rise of the morning's light,
--such is the mood of another era before her season ending storm of
sorrow. So resigned is her will (to cease to ere behold again the sight of
another begotten leaf at play upon a new mowed lawn of green, with
her sister oaks looming high above to provide the shade for another
springtime hope of another sunny day) --she lifts her limbs up high as if
to pray for one last test, for one more day; with a humble sway she
bows her head to receive her due, a rogue wind from an unseasonable
front, laced with a host of whirling gusts for her final fate of one
horrendous tornatic punch. This old oak was once like you and me,
content to abort her leaves before the rain, before the name of the Lord
became the only way to confront the loss of those perilous trials we've
endured in life, so designed to divert our ways. But now we see and
recognize that all that's left of the serpent's skin are flakes of forgiven
sin to be whisked away by the wind of another early spring. Days like
leaves will come and go, but the Lord we know as our Oak of Life,
whose roots are deep within the sod will forever draw His strength to
renew his natural and grafted branches with all their multitudes of
new-born leaves of green, never to be let go, never to be forsaken.

Originally I was born in Dearborn Michigan, but somehow at the age of two, I found myself in Beeville, Texas where I was adopted by Mr. and Mrs. P.O. Carlson who I might add are two of the finest people ever. They gave me love and a wonderful Christian up-bringing. As I look back over the years gone by, I see their guiding ways that allowed me to learn a trade, raise my family and pursue a passion for writing poems and songs, singing and recording songs and forever giving praise to my Lord and Savior JESUS CHRIST who truly made my life as it is today possible. My wife Linda and I want to thank all the good folks in Beeville that helped me along the way. My hope is that this story, poems and songs will give a sense of peace and hope to all that read these words.

NOTES

NOTES

NOTES

NOTES

NOTES

NOTES

NOTES

NOTES

NOTES

NOTES

NOTES

NOTES

NOTES

NOTES

NOTES

NOTES

NOTES

NOTES

NOTES

NOTES

NOTES

NOTES

NOTES

NOTES

Printed in the United States
By Bookmasters